Maker Faire

by Samantha Roslund and
Kristin Fontichiaro

CHERRY LAKE PUBLISHING • ANN ARBOR, MICHIGAN

A Note to Adults: Please review the instructions for the activities in this book before allowing children to do them. Be sure to help them with any activities you do not think they can safely complete on their own.

A Note to Kids: Be sure to ask an adult for help with these activities when you need it. Always put your safety first!

Published in the United States of America by Cherry Lake Publishing
Ann Arbor, Michigan
www.cherrylakepublishing.com

Series Editor: Kristin Fontichiaro
Photo Credits: Cover and pages 1, 5, and 29, ©jurvetson/www.flickr.com/ CC-BY-2.0; page 6, ©Athlex/www.flickr.com/CC-BY-2.0; pages 9 and 16, courtesy of Michigan Makers; page 13, ©tvol/www.flickr.com/CC-BY-2.0; page 14, courtesy of Quinton de Klerk; pages 18 and 20, ©Schmarty/ www.flickr.com/CC-BY-2.0; pages 19, 23, and 24, courtesy of the authors; page 26, Library of Congress Prints and Photographs Division; page 27, ©Raymond "Peaceray" Leonard/commons.wikimedia.org/CC-BY-3.0

Library of Congress Cataloging-in-Publication Data
Roslund, Samantha.
  Maker faire/by Samantha Roslund and Kristin Fontichiaro..
     pages cm.—(Makers as innovators) (Innovation library)
  Includes bibliographical references and index.
  Audience: Grade 4 to 6.
  ISBN 978-1-62431-136-9 (lib. bdg.)—ISBN 978-1-62431-202-1 (e-book)—
ISBN 978-1-62431-268-7 (pbk.)
  1. Trade shows—Juvenile literature. 2. Inventions—Juvenile literature.
I. Fontichiaro, Kristin. II. Title.
  T396.R67 2013
  607'.34—dc23   2013004921

Cherry Lake Publishing would like to acknowledge the work of The Partnership for 21st Century Skills. Please visit www.p21.org for more information.

Printed in the United States of America
Corporate Graphics Inc.
July 2013
CLFA13

21st Century Skills INNOVATION LIBRARY

Contents

Chapter 1

Makers, Makers Everywhere!

Imagine a place where it's totally normal to shoot rockets, see robots do backflips, and feel the heat of fire-breathing sculptures. It is a place where some people travel by unicycle, while others wearing lab coats and safety glasses drop candy into bottles of soda, setting off fountains of bubbles in time to music. From T-shirt silk-screening to dinosaurs made out of scrap metal, there's something to tickle your imagination at every turn. As you wander through tents, you watch machines sew designs onto cloth, kids learn to solder, and a robot carve blocks of wood into toys. Everywhere you go people are eager to show you what they're doing. Sometimes you can even take a turn at making stuff yourself! Where are you? You're at a Maker Faire!

For hundreds of years, people have come together at special events to chat, share, show off, learn, and enjoy one another's company. Over the centuries, these events have taken many names. They include expositions, market days, and fairs.

A Maker Faire is a modern version of those historic events. It combines the old term *faire* with the new term *maker*, a person who invents, creates, or fabricates something. The people at *Make* magazine run or license these events around the country. A Maker Faire is part **exhibition**, part learning workshop, and part celebration. It's a place where imagination is prized

Presenters at a Maker Faire in Queens, New York, used Mentos candies to make soda shoot from bottles into the air.

A Jeep covered in Legos? Why not? It's a Maker Faire!

above all. Everyone is welcome at a Maker Faire. Whether you're there to admire, to learn, or to share, you are a valuable addition to a Maker Faire.

You can find Maker Faires all across the globe. They began in places that were famous for being hubs of invention. The very first Maker Faire was held in 2006 in California. They have also been held in places such as New York City; Austin, Texas; Detroit, Michigan; Kansas City, Missouri; Atlanta, Georgia; and

Seattle, Washington. Some are located in foreign countries. Some Maker Faires are big-budget, multiday events. Others, known as Mini Maker Faires, take place only on a Saturday. Maker Faires of all sizes have two things in common: makers and people who enjoy seeing what makers create.

Who Are the Makers at the Maker Faire?

There are as many different types of makers at a Maker Faire as there are inventions in the world! There are individual makers with one or two creations to show off. Some makers come in groups with several people working on larger projects. Some makers are **amateurs**. Others make things for a living. Makers also have a wide range of experience. Some have just started to learn about the field in which they work, while others may have been at it for decades. At the 2012 Maker Faire in New York City, more than 60 percent of the people there had never visited a Maker Faire before. The people behind Maker Faire think that anyone can become a maker. Maker Faire founder Dale Dougherty has said, "I believe we are all makers. We can find all kinds of makers in our communities."

Makers can be welders, carpenters, stitchers, or weavers. They can be engineers, electrical wizards, potters, designers, or architects. They might work in hot factories or air-conditioned offices. Look at some of the things on your desk. Makers have probably attempted to make, update, or upgrade almost everything you see—including the desk itself! Some makers **manipulate** computers, software, electronics, and lasers. Think about the stuff in your house. Makers create, remake, or redesign appliances, clothing, and video games. They work on TVs, bikes, cars, musical instruments, and more. These are just some of the inventions and improvements that makers bring to the events to show off and share.

Working Together

Some makers work alone. Others like spending time in teams or **interest groups**. These groups might meet regularly to work on their shared interests such as pottery, *Star Wars* crafts, or lock picking. Some makers belong to the same **makerspace**, where they work in the same building but not necessarily on similar projects.

You'll find many makers sitting at shaded tables or tents at a Maker Faire, but some people need more space to showcase their creations. Keep your eyes open for street performers! They may be carrying a special prop, wearing an original costume, or driving a one-of-a-kind car, bike, or other moving invention. These people will walk around and chat with people. Feel free to ask them about their projects!

These makers created an incredible bicycle built for two. They spun around the 2012 Detroit Maker Faire to show off their hard work.

Have you ever spent a long time on a project, making something that you were really proud of? You want to show it off to your family and friends, right? But after they see it, the sharing is over. That's the great thing about Maker Faires. They're events built around sharing. There are hundreds, or sometimes thousands, of people who come specifically to look at your invention and talk to you about your work. Many of them may have questions or suggestions that could be really helpful to you and your project.

The Maker Faire spirit is one in which everyone is curious, respectful, and positive about what's being exhibited. Leave judgment and embarrassment at the event gates. The people involved in setting up and hosting Maker Faires work hard to create an environment that is friendly and welcoming.

Many people begin their Maker Faire experience as a visitor. Later, they may volunteer and eventually become **exhibitors**! Let's take a look at the different ways you can get involved in a Maker Faire.

Chapter 2

Visiting a Maker Faire

Maker Faires are not museums! You don't have to be quiet, tiptoe, and keep your hands off. You can touch or try things, and the makers hope you will. Just keep an eye out for Please Don't Touch signs posted on certain delicate or valuable items. Makers like to talk about their projects, answer your questions, and hear your ideas for **modifying** their inventions. Don't be afraid to ask them questions about your own projects. They may know of tools, resources, or **techniques** that can help you. Makers are also good connections to your maker community. They can get you in touch with other people in the area who have similar interests and projects.

Because you're going to get lots of inspiration at a Maker Faire, bring a camera so you can quickly document your experiences and observations. With so much to see, it's hard to keep track of everything.

Photographs are an easy way to remember. Cameras often capture things that you didn't notice at the time. Taking still photographs of signs and business cards will help you remember who created what. Videos can capture inventions in motion. You can also use video to record your voice as you narrate what you are filming. If you're looking around for new ideas and possible projects you'd like to start, taking a picture of something is a good way to look at an invention **holistically**.

In addition to a camera, you'll want to arrive prepared for the weather, as most Maker Faires take place outside. You'll be standing on concrete for most of the day. Be sure to wear comfortable shoes. Drink plenty of water and wear sunscreen!

Getting Involved in the Fun

Maker Faires aren't just for seeing what people have already made. There are many free or inexpensive hands-on activities that you can do. Some of those activities may involve working with power tools, making a craft, turning a power crank, or participating in a demonstration. If there are safety concerns for an

Robots might be a strange sight in most places, but they are common at Maker Faires.

activity, your parent or guardian might be asked to sign a **consent form** before you can participate. After the form is signed, you will receive a wristband that tells event organizers that you have permission to take part.

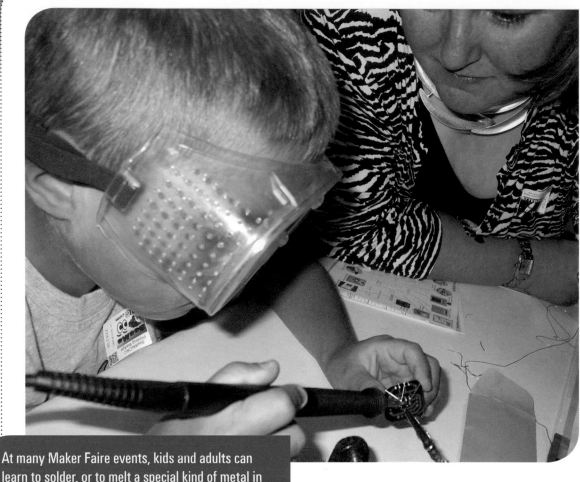

At many Maker Faire events, kids and adults can learn to solder, or to melt a special kind of metal in order to connect wires together.

Visiting the Maker Shed

At large Maker Faires, keep your eyes open for the Maker Shed. (It's usually a tent, not a shed!) Inside, visitors can check out and purchase hundreds of different products that range from electronic components to computer and cell phone accessories and much more. There might be personal 3D printer kits, rocket blasters, and glow-in-the-dark putty! There are also workshops that anyone with an activity wristband can join. One common activity is a soldering workshop.

Turn Your Maker Faire Trip into a Field Trip

Maker Faires are more fun with a group! If your family and friends aren't able to go with you, talk to your teachers or school librarian and ask if they would be interested in setting up a field trip. Do a little research before you ask, so you have information to show them when you make the suggestion. Visit the Web site of your local Maker Faire or call the people responsible for setting it up. Don't be shy. It's their job to inform you about all the possibilities the event has to offer. Ask about the following details:

- dates and times of the Maker Faire
- special activities or discounts for groups
- the location of the group entrance
- where to park
- ticket prices and other costs

The activities you do at school can give you ideas for what to share at a Maker Faire.

If you help adults find answers to these questions, it will be easier for them to organize a group trip. Try to connect the activities happening at the Maker Faire to what you are studying in school or working on in a club.

Chapter 3

Being a Maker Faire Volunteer

Once you're hooked on Maker Faires, why not volunteer? Volunteers at Maker Faires get all the advantages of attendees plus a behind-the-scenes look at all that goes on there. You can usually identify volunteers at a Maker Faire by their special T-shirts. If you plan to volunteer, you may spend time with the exhibitors. For example, some volunteers get to help set up props for a popular event during which Mentos candies are dropped in bottles of soda pop, creating huge fountains!

Other volunteers help set up the Maker Shed and get a closer look at all the merchandise before the crowds start walking through. Volunteers help at the information booth, and they help set up and **strike** the event. As a volunteer, you might get to be an assistant, helping makers in their tents. You might help with an

Sometimes at a Maker Faire, you get to meet a maker celebrity, like Bre Pettis, cofounder of the Makerbot 3D printer company!

activity, keep an eye on things, and answer questions while the makers go on break or are busy with other people. Some volunteers also help out with general errands, crowd control, parking, and safety.

If you volunteer, you'll not only have fun, but you'll also learn a lot more about how things work at a Maker Faire. This is important if you've ever thought about putting on your own Maker Faire. Getting to know more about the inner workings of the event will make planning your own that much easier. To learn more about volunteering, check out the online hand-book at *www.makerfaire.com*.

Makers at this booth at the 2012 Detroit Maker Faire created a giant version of the popular board game Operation. Visitors take turns trying to pull objects out of holes cut into plywood without touching the metal linings and hearing a loud "zap."

Chapter 4

Exhibiting at a Maker Faire

Makers are always makers, regardless of whether or not they're participating in a Maker Faire. But the point of showing your work at a Maker Faire is to share it with the community, interact with other makers, and learn from one another.

Presenters put a lot of effort into getting their projects ready to display at Maker Faires.

At Maker Faires, the makers who reserve table or tent display space are called exhibitors. The word *exhibitors* includes the root word *exhibit*, which means "to show or display." To exhibit at a Maker Faire, submit an application on the event's Web site. The application will probably be found in the drop-down menu under the How To Participate tab. It will ask you if you are planning to take part as a maker, a music performer, or a presenter. It will also ask you to write a brief description about what you want to exhibit. You can include the address for a Web site you created about your invention and submit photos so that the organizers of the Maker Faire can see what you've been working on.

Keep in mind that you can exhibit alone or as part of a group. Some of the best makers exhibit creations that the public can interact with or that focus on the process the creators used to build them. This allows people to see all the work that went into the production.

Are You Nervous About Showing Off Your Project?
Do you feel a little shy or weird about showing off a creation or invention at a Maker Faire? Sometimes

it can feel a little intimidating to put something you made on display for a lot of people to look at and talk about. It might feel a little like you're putting yourself on display. You might worry that people won't like it or won't get as excited about it as you are. That can feel scary. It's important to remember a few things:

- **People are very supportive at Maker Faires.** Criticism and negativity are majorly frowned upon at Maker Faires. Most people are there to give you positive feedback and encourage you.

- **Being a part of a group can really help.** Signing up to exhibit with friends or class-mates can give you courage.

- **Experts are there to support you.** Some people who stop by your tent might have greater knowledge than you do about your topic or area of interest. Don't be intimidated! Take advantage of their expertise. Ask questions, swap ideas, and ask for contact information. These people might live nearby and be a great help with your future projects.

During the Maker Faire, you will probably be in a tent with other exhibitors. When you don't have visitors, enjoy the chance to chat with your neighbors!

Turn It Up!

It's fun to share your inventions with Maker Faire visitors. At the Detroit Maker Faire in June 2012, Devin Hauersperger of Kettering University in Flint, Michigan, showed off a suitcase and a guitar case converted into iPod speakers.

At the 2012 Detroit Maker Faire, kids experimented with giant bubbles at a station that provided different types of bubble makers, soapy water, and a lot of fun. Often, Maker Faires have interactive stations like this one that allow visitors a chance to work with and try out different inventions.

Chapter 5

Hosting a Mini Maker Faire

If being a part of a large Maker Faire is fun, why not consider organizing and hosting your own Maker Faire at school, in your neighborhood, or in your scouting or hobby group?

Most people begin by partnering with others to put on a local Mini Maker Faire. If you want to use the term Maker Faire in your event name, you'll need to get permission. Visit *http://makerfaire.com/mini/* to learn the details of how to do that.

As you plan your event, you'll need a committee of other committed volunteers to help you. There are many things you'll need to think about:

- **Publicity.** How will people find out about your Maker Faire? How much will promoting the event cost? Who could help you spread the word for free?
- **Budget.** How will you pay for the tents, tables, T-shirts, and venue rental? How much will you have to charge for tickets to break even?

Fairs Throughout History

The Maker Faire phenomenon is relatively new, but people have been coming together for centuries to trade goods, share information, and show off their creations. Hundreds of years ago, farmers and artisans held weekly market days. People who needed groceries, a new broom, or a new ceramic plate could find them at market day. State fairs offer opportunities for quilters, farmers, cooks, weavers, and creators to show off their wares. From the late 1800s through the late 20th century, it was exciting to visit a world's fair to encounter the latest inventions, taste the newest and most exotic foods, and see art, culture, and science from around the world.

At the Chicago World's Fair of 1893, formally known as the World's Columbian Exposition, the organizers built a small city of buildings. Visitors were thrilled to see new creations like the first Ferris wheel, Aunt Jemima syrup, ice cream cones, Cracker Jack candy, Cream of Wheat cereal, Juicy Fruit gum, and an automatic dishwasher. Today, these inventions are familiar to millions of people. But there was a time when they were the latest and greatest!

Today, the Chicago Museum of Science and Industry is the only building left from the 1893 Chicago World's Fair. When you visit the museum, you're connected to a long history of people showing off their inventions and creations!

This maker built a hat out of toothpicks.

- **Safety.** Which events require safety precautions, such as safety glasses or fire extinguishers?
- **Power.** Many inventions need to be plugged in. Do you have enough power outlets? How many extension cords do you need? Ask the building custodian or facilities manager for help.
- **Layout.** How will you arrange the tables and tents? Which doors will be the entrances?

Which will be the exits? How will you arrange the event so that attendees can get a chance to see everything?

- **Exhibitors.** Who will bring and share their inventions? How will you find them and communicate with them?
- **Demonstrations and Education.** Who can host workshops, demonstrations, or other educational activities?
- **Food and Beverages.** When people get hungry or thirsty, will they have to leave the event? Will you have concessions?
- **Facilities.** Do you have enough bathrooms? Do you need to rent outdoor toilets?
- **Sales.** Will you sell hobby kits and T-shirts? How will you calculate a fair price that covers your expenses but is still reasonable for the customer?

Remember, the maker community is a generous one, so reach out to local makerspaces, craft guilds, workshops, and hackerspaces. Someone there may be interested in partnering with you!

A Maker Faire is a fun way to explore, share, and get in touch with your community. No matter how you choose to participate, a Maker Faire is one of the best ways to share your creations with your community and get the feedback that is so important to all makers. How can we learn and make progress if we don't talk to one another and offer help?

After you've attended one or two Maker Faires, you'll know all about the open, comfortable, and creative energy and attitudes that the participants have. It's contagious!

You never know what you'll see at a Maker Faire!

Glossary

amateurs (AM-uh-churz) people who perform skills or activities nonprofessionally

consent form (kuhn-SENT FORM) a permission slip signed by a parent or guardian that allows a person to participate in activities that may require safety precautions or adult supervision

exhibition (ek-suh-BISH-un) a public display of things that interest people

exhibitors (ek-ZIB-uh-turz) people displaying their work to the public

holistically (hoh-LIS-tik-lee) considering something as a whole rather than a collection of small parts

interest groups (IN-trist GROOPS) makers who meet regularly to work on similar interests or who belong to the same makerspace

makerspace (MAY-kur-spays) a place where makers come together to make, tinker, invent, and share

manipulate (muh-NIP-yuh-late) to change, reshape, or modify a creation

modifying (MAH-duh-fye-ing) changing something in order to make it better or more useful

strike (STRIKE) to take down tents, help load trucks and vans, and do general cleanup at the end of an event

techniques (tek-NEEKS) ways of doing something

Find Out More

BOOKS

Alter, Judy. *Meet Me at the Fair: County, State, and World's Fairs & Expositions.* New York: Franklin Watts, 1997.

Nelson, David Erik. *Snip, Burn, Solder, Shred: Seriously Geeky Stuff to Make With Your Kids.* San Francisco: No Starch Press, 2011.

WEB SITES

Instructables
www.instructables.com
Find instructions for how to build lots of cool stuff.

Maker Faire
www.makerfaire.com
Learn about the dates, locations, and guidelines of Maker Faire events and how you can participate as an attendee, volunteer, or maker.

Make: Kids & Family
http://blog.makezine.com/kids
Find lots of cool, kid-friendly stuff you can make, often using things you have around the house already!

Index

About the Authors

Kristin Fontichiaro (left) teaches at the University of Michigan and works with the Michigan Makers team.

Samantha Roslund (right) is a school library media master's student at the University of Michigan and helped develop Michigan Makers (*http://michiganmakers.webly.com/*), an after-school program for young makers.